I
AM

103 Tips to Becoming Your True Self

Dr. Katherine Y. Brown

I0519163

www.TrueVinePublishing.org

I Am Authentic
Dr. Katherine Y. Brown

Published by True Vine Publishing Co.
810 Dominican Dr.
Nashville, TN 37228
www.TrueVinePublishing.org

ISBN: 978-1-962783-33-0 Paperback
ISBN: 978-1-962783-31-6 eBook

Printed in the United States of America—First printing

Table of Contents

Dedication

This book is dedicated to everyone who dares to dream despite life's obstacles. The world is waiting on you and will not be the same unless you complete the assignment that only you were created to do.

-Dr. Katherine Y. Brown

Introduction

My life journey has been remarkably unique, encompassing moments of both success and failure, each serving as valuable opportunities for self-reflection and personal growth. Throughout my experiences, I have come to realize that people often conceal the truth of their own journeys. Relying on others' seemingly successful paths may lead to a skewed perception of success, as they may not be authentically expressing their true selves. Consequently, this disparity can result in internal conflict and challenges when achieving a level of success based solely on observation, only to discover that it does not bring true happiness.

To address this unspoken truth, it is crucial to turn inward and uncover your own truth. Have you taken the time to pause and reflect on what truly brings you happiness? Your personal journey toward discovering your truth is inherently unique, and it is solely within your power to determine the path you are willing to pursue.

In this book, I have compiled a collection of reflections presented as quotes and thought-provoking questions that have played a significant role in the pursuit of truth.

Whose truth are we seeking?

Perhaps these pages will help you to identify your own truth, or they may deeply resonate with someone close to you, prompting you to share this guide with them. Each page provides an opportunity to pause for reflection, contemplation and exploration on the road to embrace your authentic self. In a world filled with options, your decision to invest your time in reading these words is appreciated.

Embrace the Process

This book serves as a guide, adaptable to suit your individual needs in the present moment. Whether you choose to read it in one sitting or prefer to take a more deliberate approach of absorbing a single page each day, followed by journaling and reflection, what matters most is that you embrace the process.

Furthermore, an opportunity awaits for you to share your personal journey with others. Consider reading a page within a group setting and engaging in dialogue, allowing each participant to reflect upon the quotes, questions, and discussions through their unique lens and lived experiences. The choice is yours. Remember, this book is a tool, and you are the empowered user.

The possibilities before you are endless, intentionally designed to be so. Authentic living knows no bounds; therefore, do not confine yourself. You possess numerous avenues to explore and utilize this book. Speak your truth. Seek your truth. Define your truth. Embrace and own your truth. There is no singular approach to navigating the concepts presented within these pages.

- Question
- Explore
- Inspire
- Discuss

Embrace and own your journey.

Explore the depths of your truth.

Part I:

PERSONAL DEVELOPMENT AND SELF-IMPROVEMENT

TIP 1:

SET YOUR FOUNDATION

Memorize quotes that deeply resonate with you. Quotes have the power to ignite inspiration and serve as touchstones along your journey through life. They can be a source of guidance, comfort, and motivation. Take the time to find quotes that truly speak to your soul and commit them to memory. Whenever you need a boost or a moment of reflection, let these words be your foundation.

How can the incorporation meaningful quotes into your daily life help you to stay motivated, inspired, and focused on your personal and professional goals?

_____

_____

_____

TIP 2:
CULTIVATE A GROWTH MINDSET

Develop a growth mindset to embrace challenges and view failures as opportunities to learn. A growth mindset helps you to adapt to change while remaining open to feedback and new ideas. Embrace the belief that your abilities and intelligence can be developed through dedication and hard work. Approach tasks with curiosity, persistence, and a willingness to step outside of your comfort zone.

How can cultivating a growth mindset help you to overcome obstacles, achieve personal and professional growth, and unlock your full potential?

_____

_____

_____

TIP 3:
PRACTICE SELF-REFLECTION

Take time for self-reflection to gain a deeper understanding of yourself and your experiences. Set aside regular moments of solitude to examine your thoughts, feelings, and actions. Ask yourself meaningful questions about your values, goals, and aspirations. Self-reflection enhances self-awareness and helps you to to make conscious choices that are aligned with your authentic self.

How can incorporating regular self-reflection practices into your life help you to make better decisions, align your actions with your values, and foster personal growth?

_____

_____

_____

TIP 4:
EMBRACE CONTINUOUS LEARNING

Commit to lifelong learning to stay intellectually curious and adaptable in a rapidly changing world. Seek out new knowledge, acquire new skills, and expose yourself to diverse perspectives. Embrace learning opportunities from various sources such as books, courses, workshops, and interactions with others. Continually expanding your knowledge base enables personal and professional growth.

How can adopting a mindset of continuous learning enhance your leadership abilities, broaden your perspectives, and contribute to your personal and professional success?

_____

_____

_____

Part II:

ENHANCING EMOTIONAL AND
SOCIAL INTELLIGENCE

Tip 5:

Develop Emotional Intelligence

Cultivate emotional intelligence to understand and manage your emotions and the emotions of others. Emotional intelligence encompasses self-awareness, self-regulation, empathy, and effective interpersonal skills. Develop the ability to recognize and regulate your emotions, empathize with others, and build positive relationships. Emotional intelligence strengthens your leadership capabilities and fosters harmonious connections.

How can the development of emotional intelligence help you to navigate challenging situations, build strong relationships, and effectively lead and inspire others?

_____

_____

_____

TIP 6:
NURTURE RESILIENCE

Cultivate resilience to bounce back from setbacks and adapt to adversity. Resilience involves developing a mindset that views failures and obstacles as opportunities for learning and growth. Build inner strength, determination, and perseverance to face challenges with resilience. Embrace setbacks as temporary and learn from them to become stronger and more resilient.

How can nurturing resilience help you to overcome obstacles, cope with stress and change, and maintain a positive mindset in the face of adversity?

_____

_____

_____

TIP 7:
ESTABLISH BOUNDARIES FOR
EMOTIONAL WELL-BEING

Establishing boundaries is crucial for safeguarding your emotional well-being. Recognize your limits and communicate them effectively. Learn to say no and prioritize activities that bring you joy and fulfillment. By setting healthy boundaries, you create space for self-care, reduce stress, and maintain a positive emotional state.

How can you establish and communicate boundaries effectively to protect your emotional well-being and ensure a healthy work-life balance? What strategies can you employ to prioritize self-care and maintain a positive emotional state?

———————————————

———————————————

———————————————

Tip 8:
Cultivate a Positive Mindset

Develop and maintain a positive mindset to approach life's challenges with optimism and resilience. Focus on the possibilities and opportunities that lie ahead rather than dwelling on negativity. Practice gratitude, affirmations, and positive self-talk to shift your perspective and cultivate a positive outlook. A positive mindset empowers you to overcome obstacles and create a more fulfilling life.

How can the cultivation of a positive mindset enhance your overall well-being, improve your relationships, and increase your chances of success?

_____

_____

_____

TIP 9:

SET AUTHENTIC GOALS

Set goals that align with your values, passions, and purpose. Authentic goals reflect your true desires and aspirations, allowing you to pursue what truly matters to you. Define your goals with clarity and specificity, ensure that they are meaningful and inspirational. When your goals are authentic, you are more likely to stay committed, motivated, and fulfilled on your journey.

How can setting authentic goals helps you to create a sense of purpose, prioritize your actions, and lead a more fulfilling life?

TIP 10:
PRACTICE GRATITUDE

Cultivate a habit of gratitude to appreciate the positive aspects of your life. Regularly acknowledge and express gratitude for the blessings you've been given, the experiences you've had, and the relationships you've cultivated. Keep a gratitude journal where you write down three things you are grateful for each day. Gratitude shifts your focus toward abundance and promotes a more joyful and contented mindset.

How can practicing gratitude enhance your overall well-being, improve your relationships, and foster a positive outlook on life?

_____

_____

_____

TIP 11:
FOSTER HEALTHY HABITS

Develop and maintain healthy habits that support your physical, mental, and emotional well-being. Establish a routine that includes regular exercise, nutritious eating, sufficient sleep, and stress-reducing activities. Prioritize self-care and make conscious choices that nourish your body and mind. Healthy habits contribute to your overall vitality and resilience.

How can fostering healthy habits positively impact your energy levels, productivity, and overall quality of life?

_____

_____

_____

Tip 12:
Embrace Authenticity

Embrace your true self and live authentically, aligning your actions with your values and beliefs. Be honest with yourself and others, expressing your thoughts and feelings in a genuine way. Embracing authenticity fosters genuine connections, builds trust, and allows you to live a more fulfilling and meaningful life.

How can embracing authenticity in your thoughts, words, and actions enhance your relationships, personal satisfaction, and overall well-being?

_____

_____

_____

TIP 13:
DEVELOP EFFECTIVE COMMUNICATION SKILLS

Invest in developing effective communication skills to express yourself clearly, listen attentively, and convey your message in an impactful way. Enhance your verbal and nonverbal communication abilities, including active listening, empathy, and assertiveness. Effective communication builds stronger relationships, resolves conflicts, and promotes collaboration.

How can developing effective communication skills improve your personal and professional relationships, influence others positively, and lead to better outcomes in your interactions?

_____

_____

_____

TIP 14:
PRACTICE ACTIVE LISTENING

Engage in active listening to fully understand others and demonstrate respect and empathy. Give your full attention, maintain eye contact, and provide verbal and nonverbal cues to show your interest. Avoid interrupting and listen without judgment. Active listening fosters deeper connections, minimizes misunderstandings, and strengthens relationships.

How can practicing active listening enhance your ability to understand others' perspectives, build trust, and improve your communication effectiveness?

_____

_____

_____

TIP 15:

CULTIVATE EMPATHY

Develop empathy, the ability to understand and share the feelings of others. Put yourself in others' shoes, acknowledge their emotions, and respond with compassion. Cultivating empathy fosters stronger relationships, effective collaboration, and a deeper sense of connection with others.

How can cultivating empathy improve your ability to relate to others, resolve conflicts, and create a more inclusive and compassionate environment?

_____

_____

_____

TIP 16:
BUILD RAPPORT AND TRUST

Build rapport with others to establish a sense of connection and trust. Show genuine interest in their thoughts, feelings, and experiences. Find common ground, ask open-ended questions, and actively listen to create a safe and supportive environment. Building rapport and trust strengthens relationships, enhances collaboration, and fosters a positive team dynamic.

How can building rapport and trust with others improve your ability to lead, influence, and create a positive impact in your personal and professional interactions?

_____

_____

_____

TIP 17:

RESOLVE CONFLICTS CONSTRUCTIVELY

Learn to manage and resolve conflicts in a constructive manner. Seek win-win solutions by actively listening, understanding and finding common ground. Practice effective communication, compromise, and use negotiation skills to find resolutions that address everyone's needs. Constructive conflict resolution fosters stronger relationships, promotes growth, and creates a harmonious environment.

How can developing conflict resolution skills help you navigate difficult situations, strengthen relationships, and create a more positive and productive work or personal environment?

_____

_____

_____

TIP 18:

EXPRESS APPRECIATION AND RECOGNITION

Express genuine appreciation and recognition for others' contributions, efforts, and achievements. Acknowledge and celebrate their successes, both big and small. Show gratitude through verbal praise, written notes, or public recognition. Expressing appreciation and recognition fosters a positive and motivating atmosphere, builds morale, and strengthens relationships.

How can expressing appreciation and recognition contribute to a positive and supportive environment, enhance team morale, and promote a culture of appreciation?

_____

_____

_____

Tip 19:

Nurture Authentic Connections

Invest in nurturing authentic connections with others by being genuine, present, and supportive. Build meaningful relationships based on trust, empathy, and shared values. Be there for others in times of need, celebrate their successes, and offer genuine support. Authentic connections enrich your life, provide a sense of belonging, and enhance your overall well-being.

How can nurturing authentic connections with others positively impact your personal happiness, sense of community, and overall fulfillment in life?

_____

_____

_____

TIP 20:
FOSTER A GROWTH MINDSET

Cultivate a growth mindset, believing that you can develop abilities and intelligence through dedication and hard work. Embrace challenges, view failures as opportunities to learn, and persist in the face of setbacks. Cultivating a growth mindset allows you to overcome obstacles, embrace continuous learning, and reach your full potential.

How can fostering a growth mindset empower you to overcome challenges, embrace learning opportunities, and achieve personal and professional growth?

_____

_____

_____

TIP 21:

CULTIVATE MINDFUL COMMUNICATION

Practice mindful communication by being fully present, attentive, and nonjudgmental in your interactions. Slow down, listen deeply, and respond consciously rather than reactively. Mindful communication promotes understanding, reduces misinterpretations, and fosters meaningful connections.

How can cultivating mindful communication enhance your ability to listen deeply, connect authentically, and create a more harmonious and enriching communication experience?

_____

_____

_____

TIP 22:
SET CLEAR AND SPECIFIC GOALS

Set clear and specific goals that provide direction and focus for your personal and professional endeavors. Clearly define what you want to achieve, why it is important to you, and how you will measure success. Setting clear and specific goals enhances motivation, improves decision-making, and increases the likelihood of successful outcomes.

How can setting clear and specific goals improve your ability to prioritize, stay motivated, and make progress toward your desired outcomes?

_____

_____

_____

TIP 23:

CREATE ACTION PLANS

Develop action plans that outline the specific steps and resources needed to achieve your goals. Break down your goals into manageable tasks, set deadlines, and identify the necessary actions and resources. Creating action plans increases your clarity, boosts your productivity, and facilitates progress toward your goals.

How can creating action plans help you to effectively execute your goals, stay organized, and make consistent progress toward your desired outcomes?

_____

_____

_____

TIP 24:
BREAK GOALS INTO SMALLER STEPS

Break down your goals into smaller, more achievable steps. By breaking goals into manageable chunks, you can maintain momentum, celebrate incremental successes, and stay motivated. Each small step brings you closer to your larger goal, making it less overwhelming and more attainable.

How can breaking down your goals into smaller steps help you to overcome procrastination, stay focused, and make steady progress toward your desired outcomes?

Part III:

LEADERSHIP AND PROFESSIONAL DEVELOPMENT

TIP 25:

STAY MOTIVATED AND PERSISTENT

Stay motivated and persistent in pursuing your goals, even when faced with challenges or setbacks. Cultivate a strong sense of determination, remind yourself of the importance of your goals, and stay focused on the long-term vision. Maintain a positive mindset, seek support when needed, and celebrate small victories along the way.

How can you maintain motivation and persistence in the face of obstacles, setbacks, or long-term goals?

_____

_____

_____

TIP 26:
EMBRACE FAILURE AS A LEARNING OPPORTUNITY

Embrace failure as a valuable learning opportunity rather than a sign of defeat. Shift your perspective to see failure as a stepping stone to growth and improvement. Analyze failures, extract lessons, and apply those insights to future endeavors. Embracing failure as a learning opportunity fuels personal growth, builds resilience, and increases the likelihood of future success.

How can embracing failure as a learning opportunity help you to overcome fear of failure, foster innovation, and continuously improve yourself?

_____

_____

_____

TIP 27:

CELEBRATE MILESTONES AND PROGRESS

Celebrate milestones and progress along your journey to acknowledge your achievements and maintain motivation. Recognize and appreciate the smaller steps you've taken toward your larger goals. Celebrating milestones not only boosts your morale but also provides an opportunity for reflection, gratitude, and recharging.

How can celebrating milestones and progress positively impact your motivation, confidence, and overall sense of achievement?

_____

_____

_____

Tip 28:

Track and Evaluate Your Progress

Regularly track and evaluate your progress toward your goals. Monitor your actions, measure outcomes, and assess the effectiveness of your strategies. Make adjustments and refinements based on the feedback and insights you gain from tracking your progress. Tracking and evaluating your progress keeps you accountable, allows for course correction, and maximizes your chances of success.

How can tracking and evaluating your progress help you to stay on track, identify areas for improvement, and optimize your efforts toward your goals?

_____

_____

_____

TIP 29:

ADAPT AND ADJUST YOUR GOALS

Be open to adapting and adjusting your goals as circumstances change or new opportunities arise. Flexibility and adaptability allow you to respond to unforeseen challenges, leverage new possibilities, and stay aligned with your evolving priorities. Regularly reassess your goals and make adjustments as needed to ensure they remain relevant and meaningful.

How can embracing flexibility and adaptability in goal setting enhance your ability to navigate uncertainty, seize opportunities, and maintain focus on what truly matters?

_____

_____

_____

TIP 30:
PRACTICE SELF-REFLECTION FOR GOAL ALIGNMENT

Engage in regular self-reflection to ensure your goals align with your values, passions, and purpose. Take time to assess whether your goals still resonate with your true desires and aspirations. Reflect on your progress, evaluate your priorities, and make any necessary adjustments to ensure your goals remain authentic and meaningful to you.

How can practicing self-reflection help you to align your goals with your core values, passions, and overall sense of purpose?

_____

_____

_____

TIP 31:
LEAD BY EXAMPLE

Lead by example by embodying the qualities and behaviors you expect from others. Model integrity, accountability, empathy, and professionalism. Show respect for others, demonstrate a strong work ethic, and maintain a positive attitude. Leading by example inspires others to follow and creates a culture of excellence and high standards.

How can leading by example positively influence the behavior, morale, and performance of those around you?

_____

_____

_____

TIP 32:
INSPIRE AND MOTIVATE OTHERS

Inspire and motivate others by sharing a compelling vision, setting clear expectations, and recognizing their contributions. Communicate your vision with passion, provide meaningful feedback and encouragement, and create a supportive environment that fosters growth and development. Inspiring and motivating others unlocks their potential, promotes engagement, and drives collective success.

How can you inspire and motivate others to achieve their full potential, go beyond their limits, and contribute to the success of the team or organization?

_____

_____

_____

TIP 33:
DELEGATE AND EMPOWER TEAM MEMBERS

Delegate tasks and responsibilities to team members to empower them and foster a sense of ownership. Clearly communicate expectations, provide necessary resources and support, and trust in their abilities. Delegating effectively allows you to focus on strategic initiatives, develop the skills of your team, and promote a culture of trust and collaboration.

How can delegating tasks and empowering team members enhance productivity, promote growth, and create a more engaged and efficient work environment?

_____

_____

_____

TIP 34:
FOSTER A COLLABORATIVE TEAM ENVIRONMENT

Create a collaborative team environment that encourages open communication, cooperation, and synergy. Encourage the sharing of ideas, diverse perspectives, and collective problem-solving. Foster a culture where everyone's input is valued and respected. A collaborative team environment fosters innovation, enhances productivity, and strengthens the sense of belonging and camaraderie.

How can you foster a collaborative team environment that promotes effective communication, harnesses the collective intelligence, and drives superior results?

_____

_____

_____

TIP 35:

PROVIDE CONSTRUCTIVE FEEDBACK

Provide constructive feedback to help others improve their performance, develop their skills, and achieve their goals. Offer feedback that is specific, timely, and actionable. Focus on behaviors and outcomes, and provide suggestions for improvement. Constructive feedback facilitates personal and professional growth, strengthens relationships, and fosters a culture of continuous improvement.

How can providing constructive feedback effectively contribute to individual development, strengthen teamwork, and drive overall improvement?

_____

_____

_____

TIP 36:
ENCOURAGE GROWTH AND DEVELOPMENT

Encourage the growth and development of your team members by providing opportunities for learning, skillbuilding, and career advancement. Support their professional development goals, offer challenging assignments, and provide guidance and mentorship. Encouraging growth and development empowers individuals, improves team performance, and cultivates a culture of continuous learning.

How can you foster an environment that encourages the growth, development, and career advancement of your team members?

_____

_____

_____

TIP 37:
LEAD WITH INTEGRITY

Lead with integrity by aligning your actions and decisions with ethical principles and core values. Demonstrate honesty, transparency, and accountability in your interactions. Build trust by following through on commitments, treating others with fairness, and upholding ethical standards. Leading with integrity creates a culture of trust, respect, and ethical behavior.

How can leading with integrity positively impact your relationships, credibility, and overall effectiveness as a leader?

_____

_____

_____

TIP 38:
FOSTER A POSITIVE WORK CULTURE

Foster a positive work culture that promotes a sense of belonging, well-being, and engagement. Create an environment where individuals feel valued, supported, and motivated. Encourage positive interactions, celebrate successes, and promote work-life balance. A positive work culture enhances morale, productivity, and employee retention.

How can you contribute to fostering a positive work culture that promotes well-being, collaboration, and overall job satisfaction?

_____

_____

_____

TIP 39:
CULTIVATE EFFECTIVE DECISION-MAKING SKILLS

Cultivate effective decision-making skills by considering relevant information, weighing pros and cons, and evaluating potential outcomes. Seek input from diverse perspectives, conduct thorough analyses, and trust your intuition. Effective decision-making facilitates problem-solving, minimizes risks, and drives results.

How can you cultivate effective decision-making skills that lead to informed choices, minimize biases, and maximize positive outcomes?

_____

_____

_____

Tip 40:
Manage Time and Priorities
Effectively

Manage your time and priorities effectively by setting clear goals, organizing tasks, and utilizing time-management techniques. Prioritize activities based on their importance and urgency, minimize distractions, and delegate tasks when possible. Effective time management allows you to increase productivity, reduce stress, and achieve a better work-life balance.

How can you improve your time management and prioritization skills to maximize productivity and minimize stress?

_____

_____

_____

TIP 41:

FOSTER INNOVATION AND CREATIVITY

Foster innovation and creativity by creating an environment that encourages experimentation, risk-taking, and open-mindedness. Support idea generation, provide resources for innovation, and promote a culture that embraces and rewards creative thinking. Fostering innovation and creativity cultivates a competitive edge, drives growth, and fosters continuous improvement.

How can you foster innovation and creativity within your team or organization to drive meaningful change and achieve breakthrough results?

_____

_____

_____

TIP 42:
FOSTER INCLUSIVE LEADERSHIP

Foster inclusive leadership by valuing diversity, promoting equity, and creating a sense of belonging for all individuals. Embrace and leverage different perspectives, ensure equal opportunities for growth, and address biases and barriers. Inclusive leadership fosters innovation, enhances decision-making, and creates a supportive and high-performing team.

How can you cultivate inclusive leadership practices that promote diversity, equity, and inclusion within your team or organization?

_____

_____

_____

TIP 43:

CULTIVATE EMOTIONAL INTELLIGENCE

Cultivate emotional intelligence to understand and manage your emotions and the emotions of others. Do this by improving your self-awareness, self-regulation, empathy, and interpersonal skills. Develop the ability to recognize and regulate your emotions, empathize with others, and build positive relationships. Emotional intelligence strengthens your leadership capabilities and fosters harmonious connections.

How can developing emotional intelligence help you to navigate challenging situations, build strong relationships, and effectively lead and inspire others?

_____

_____

_____

TIP 44:

LEAD CHANGE AND ADAPTATION

Lead change and adaptation by embracing and guiding others through periods of transition and uncertainty. Communicate the need for change, provide support, and address resistance. Foster a culture that values continuous improvement, flexibility, and resilience. By doing this, you will ensure the long-term success and sustainability of your team or organization.

How can you effectively lead change and guide others through transitions to ensure successful adaptation and continuous improvement?

_____

_____

_____

TIP 45:
FOSTER TEAM COLLABORATION AND SYNERGY

Foster team collaboration and synergy by promoting open communication, trust, and shared goals. Encourage collaboration, facilitate effective teamwork, and promote an environment that values diverse perspectives and contributions. Team collaboration and synergy lead to enhanced creativity, innovation, and collective success.

How can you foster team collaboration and synergy to achieve shared goals, maximize team performance, and create a sense of collective achievement?

_____

_____

_____

Part IV:

EFFECTIVE COMMUNICATION AND
RELATIONSHIP MANAGEMENT

TIP 46:

CULTIVATE A LEARNING ORGANIZATION

Cultivate a learning organization by creating a culture that values continuous learning, innovation, and knowledge-sharing. Encourage individuals to seek new knowledge, share insights, and apply learning to their work. Establish systems and processes that support ongoing learning and development. A learning organization thrives in a rapidly changing world and remains competitive and adaptable.

How can you cultivate a learning organization that encourages growth, fosters innovation, and supports continuous improvement?

_____

_____

_____

TIP 47:
DEVELOP HIGH-PERFORMING TEAMS

Develop high-performing teams by aligning team goals with organizational objectives, fostering open communication, and providing the necessary resources and support. Clarify roles and responsibilities, build trust, and promote a collaborative environment. Developing high-performing teams leads to increased productivity, employee satisfaction, and superior outcomes.

How can you develop high-performing teams that deliver exceptional results and contribute to organizational success?

_____

_____

_____

TIP 48:

FOSTER ETHICAL LEADERSHIP

Foster ethical leadership by upholding ethical standards, demonstrating integrity, and making ethical decisions. Lead with transparency, fairness, and honesty, and hold yourself and others accountable to ethical principles. Ethical leadership establishes trust, builds credibility, and creates a culture of integrity.

How can you foster ethical leadership and create an environment that promotes ethical behavior and decision-making?

_____

_____

_____

TIP 49:
NURTURE A GROWTH MINDSET IN OTHERS

Nurture a growth mindset in others by promoting a culture that embraces learning, effort, and resilience. Encourage individuals to take on challenges, learn from their mistakes, and believe in their capacity for growth. Provide support, feedback, and opportunities for skill development. Nurturing a growth mindset in others enhances their potential, fosters personal and professional development, and drives organizational success.

How can you nurture a growth mindset in others and create an environment that supports their continuous growth and development?

_____

_____

_____

TIP 50:

LEAD WITH EMPATHY AND COMPASSION

Lead with empathy and compassion by understanding and valuing the emotions and experiences of others. Show empathy by actively listening, validating their emotions, and providing support. Lead with compassion by demonstrating care, kindness, and understanding. Leading with empathy and compassion fosters trust, can enhance the well-being of those you work with, and creates a positive and inclusive work environment.

How can you lead with empathy and compassion to foster trust, enhance team morale, and create a supportive work environment?

_____

_____

_____

TIP 51:
DEVELOP EFFECTIVE COACHING SKILLS

Develop effective coaching skills to empower and support the growth and development of individuals. Ask powerful questions, provide constructive feedback, and offer guidance and resources. Create a safe and supportive space for learning and skill building. Effective coaching inspires individuals to reach their full potential and achieve their goals.

How can you develop effective coaching skills to help individuals unlock their potential, improve their performance, and achieve their goals?

_____

_____

_____

Part V:

STRATEGIC THINKING AND ADVANCED
PROFESSIONAL SKILLS

TIP 52:
FOSTER EMPLOYEE ENGAGEMENT AND MOTIVATION

Foster employee engagement and motivation by creating a work environment that values employees' contributions, provides growth opportunities, and recognizes achievements. Encourage autonomy, offer meaningful work, and provide regular feedback and recognition. Fostering employee engagement and motivation leads to increased job satisfaction, productivity, and organizational success.

How can you foster employee engagement and motivation to create a positive work culture and drive individual and team performance?

_____

_____

_____

TIP 53:
PROMOTE DIVERSITY AND INCLUSION

Promote diversity and inclusion by embracing and valuing individual differences, creating equitable opportunities, and ensuring a sense of belonging for all. Foster an inclusive work environment where everyone feels respected, valued, and empowered. Promoting diversity and inclusion enhances innovation, creativity, and overall organizational performance.

How can you promote diversity and inclusion within your team or organization to foster a culture of respect, equality, and innovation?

_____

_____

_____

TIP 54:
DEVELOP EFFECTIVE CONFLICT
MANAGEMENT SKILLS

Develop effective conflict management skills to address conflicts in a constructive way and find mutually beneficial resolutions. Encourage open communication, active listening, and empathy. Use conflict as an opportunity for growth and building stronger relationships. Effective conflict management enhances collaboration, strengthens teamwork, and drives positive outcomes.

How can you develop effective conflict management skills to navigate conflicts, promote healthy dialogue, and foster positive relationships in your workplace?

_____

_____

_____

TIP 55:
FOSTER WORK-LIFE INTEGRATION

Foster work-life integration by promoting a healthy balance between work responsibilities and personal well-being. Encourage flexibility, provide support for work-life balance, and prioritize self-care. Foster a culture that values the whole person and supports employees in achieving harmony between their personal and professional lives.

How can you foster work-life integration to support employee well-being, job satisfaction, and productivity?

_____

_____

_____

TIP 56:
LEAD VIRTUAL AND REMOTE TEAMS

Lead virtual and remote teams effectively by establishing clear communication channels, leveraging technology, and providing support for remote work. Foster a sense of connection, maintain regular check-ins, and promote collaboration and engagement in a virtual environment. Leading virtual and remote teams allows for flexibility, increases access to talent, and supports work-life balance.

How can you lead virtual and remote teams effectively and foster collaboration, engagement, and productivity in a remote work environment?

_____

_____

_____

TIP 57:
DEVELOP CROSS-CULTURAL COMPETENCE

Develop cross-cultural competence to effectively navigate and appreciate cultural differences. Seek to understand different cultures, customs, and perspectives. Practice empathy, adaptability, and open-mindedness in cross-cultural interactions. Developing cross-cultural competence enhances communication, collaboration, and global leadership capabilities.

How can you develop cross-cultural competence to foster understanding, bridge cultural gaps, and enhance global leadership effectiveness?

_____

_____

_____

TIP 58:
PRACTICE ETHICAL DECISION-MAKING

Practice ethical decision-making by considering the ethical implications of your choices and aligning them with ethical principles and values. Seek multiple perspectives, assess potential impacts, and choose actions that prioritize the well-being of all stakeholders. Practicing ethical decision-making upholds integrity, builds trust, and contributes to a sustainable and responsible organization.

How can you practice ethical decision-making in complex situations and contribute to a culture of ethics and responsibility?

_____

_____

_____

TIP 59:
LEAD SUSTAINABLE PRACTICES

Lead sustainable practices by integrating environmental, social, and economic considerations into your decision-making and operations. Promote responsible resource use, minimize waste, and support initiatives that contribute to a sustainable future. Leading sustainable practices demonstrates corporate social responsibility and positions your organization as a driver of positive change.

How can you lead sustainable practices to make a positive impact on the environment, society, and your organization's long-term success?

_____

_____

_____

TIP 60:

FOSTER RESILIENCE IN OTHERS

Foster resilience in others by providing support, promoting self-care, and encouraging a growth mindset. Help individuals develop coping strategies, bounce back from setbacks, and adapt to change. Fostering resilience in others enhances their ability to navigate challenges, maintain their well-being, and achieve long-term success.

How can you foster resilience in others to support their well-being, growth, and ability to overcome obstacles?

_____

_____

_____

TIP 61:
DEVELOP EFFECTIVE PRESENTATION SKILLS

Develop effective presentation skills to communicate your ideas, influence others, and deliver compelling presentations. Practice public speaking, prepare engaging visuals, and hone your delivery style. These skills will enhance your ability to inform, inspire, and engage your audience.

How can developing effective presentation skills help you to deliver impactful presentations and effectively communicate your message to diverse audiences?

_____

_____

_____

TIP 62:

ENHANCE NEGOTIATION SKILLS

Enhance your negotiation skills to achieve win-win outcomes, build stronger relationships, and resolve conflicts effectively. Prepare thoroughly, listen actively, and seek creative solutions. Maintain a collaborative and principled approach that focuses on shared interests and mutual benefit. Enhancing negotiation skills improves your ability to reach agreements that satisfy all parties involved.

How can enhancing your negotiation skills contribute to more successful outcomes, improved relationships, and effective conflict resolution?

_____

_____

_____

TIP 63:
DEVELOP FINANCIAL LITERACY

Develop financial literacy to understand and manage your personal and professional finances effectively. Learn about budgeting, investments, financial planning, and risk management. Developing financial literacy empowers you to make informed decisions, secure your financial future, and achieve financial well-being.

How can developing financial literacy improve your ability to make sound financial decisions, create financial stability, and pursue your financial goals?

_____

_____

_____

TIP 64:

CULTIVATE AN INNOVATION MINDSET

Cultivate an innovation mindset by embracing curiosity and ambiguity, and by challenging conventional thinking. Encourage experimentation, tolerate failure, and promote a culture that rewards innovation. Cultivating an innovation mindset fosters creativity, drives continuous improvement, and positions you as a forward-thinking leader.

How can you cultivate an innovation mindset that promotes creativity, fosters problem-solving, and drives organizational success?

TIP 65:
DEVELOP CROSS-FUNCTIONAL COLLABORATION SKILLS

Develop cross-functional collaboration skills to effectively work with individuals from different departments or areas of expertise. Foster relationships, seek diverse perspectives, and collaborate on projects that require interdisciplinary cooperation. Developing cross-functional collaboration skills enhances communication, breaks down silos, and fosters a culture of collaboration.

How can developing cross-functional collaboration skills contribute to improved teamwork, organizational efficiency, and better outcomes?

_____

_____

_____

TIP 66:
DEVELOP EFFECTIVE STAKEHOLDER MANAGEMENT

Develop effective stakeholder management skills to identify, understand, and engage with individuals or groups who have an interest in your work. Prioritize stakeholder needs, build relationships, and communicate effectively to gain support and achieve mutually beneficial outcomes. Effective stakeholder management strengthens partnerships, minimizes conflicts, and drives project success.

How can developing effective stakeholder management skills improve your ability to engage stakeholders, build strong relationships, and achieve project success?

_____

_____

_____

TIP 67:
CULTIVATE STRATEGIC THINKING

Cultivate strategic thinking to analyze complex situations, anticipate trends, and make informed decisions aligned with long-term goals. Develop a broader perspective, consider multiple scenarios, and evaluate potential risks and opportunities. Cultivating strategic thinking enhances your ability to navigate uncertainty, make sound decisions, and lead with foresight.

How can cultivating strategic thinking enhance your ability to identify strategic opportunities, adapt to change, and make informed decisions?

_____

_____

_____

TIP 68:

DEVELOP EFFECTIVE NETWORKING SKILLS

Develop effective networking skills to build and nurture relationships that support your personal and professional growth. Attend industry events, connect with professionals in your field, and leverage online networking platforms. Be authentic, show genuine interest, and offer value to others. Developing these skills will help you to expand your professional network, open doors to opportunities, and foster career advancement.

How can developing effective networking skills help you to build valuable connections, access new opportunities, and advance in your career?

_____

_____

_____

TIP 69:
PROMOTE MENTAL HEALTH AND WELL-BEING

Promote mental health and well-being by creating a supportive work environment that values mental well-being, offers resources for support, and reduces stigma. Encourage work-life balance, provide access to mental health resources, and promote self-care. Promoting mental health and well-being enhances employee satisfaction, productivity, and the overall success of your organization.

How can you promote mental health and well-being within your team or organization to create a supportive and thriving work environment?

_____

_____

_____

TIP 70:

LEAD WITH CULTURAL INTELLIGENCE

Lead with cultural intelligence by understanding and respecting cultural differences, adapting your leadership style, and leveraging diversity as a strength. Seek to understand different cultural norms, customs, and communication styles. Leading with cultural intelligence enhances your ability to lead diverse teams, build global relationships, and drive cross-cultural collaboration.

How can you lead with cultural intelligence to promote inclusivity, strengthen relationships, and enhance leadership effectiveness in a multicultural environment?

_____

_____

_____

Tip 71:
Develop Resonant Leadership

Develop resonant leadership by cultivating self-awareness, empathy, and authenticity. Build deep connections with others, inspire and motivate through your actions and words, and create a positive emotional climate. Resonant leadership fosters trust, engagement, and a sense of purpose among your team or organization.

How can you develop resonant leadership to create an environment where individuals thrive, relationships flourish, and your organization achieves its goals?

_____

_____

_____

FOSTER DATA-DRIVEN DECISION-MAKING

Foster data-driven decision-making by using data and analytics to inform your choices and actions. Collect and analyze relevant data, draw insights, and make informed decisions based on evidence. Foster a culture that values data, promotes data literacy, and encourages fact-based decision-making. Fostering data-driven decision-making improves your ability to drive efficiency, identify trends, and achieve better outcomes.

How can fostering data-driven decision-making help you to make more informed choices, improve organizational performance, and drive innovation?

TIP 73:
DEVELOP CRISIS MANAGEMENT SKILLS

Develop crisis management skills to effectively navigate crises when they occur. Anticipate potential risks, develop contingency plans, and establish clear communication channels. Remain calm, take decisive action, and provide support to those affected. Developing crisis management skills allows you to respond effectively, minimize damage, and restore stability in challenging situations.

How can developing crisis management skills help you to respond effectively to crises, protect your team or organization, and ensure continuity in challenging times?

_____

_____

_____

TIP 74:
SURROUND YOURSELF WITH
SUPPORTERS AND MENTORS

Surround yourself with individuals who believe in your goals and aspirations. Seek out mentors who can provide guidance, support, and encouragement on your journey. Surrounding yourself with positive influences help you to stay focused, motivated, and resilient, even when faced with challenges or negative influences.

How can you actively seek out supporters and mentors who will uplift and empower you on your path to success?

_____

_____

_____

TIP 75:
LEAD WITH AUTHENTICITY
AND VULNERABILITY

Lead with authenticity and vulnerability by being true to yourself, acknowledging your limitations, and being open about your emotions and experiences. Share your journey, show vulnerability, and create a safe space for others to do the same. Leading with authenticity and vulnerability builds trust, fosters meaningful connections, and promotes a culture of authenticity.

How can leading with authenticity and vulnerability positively impact your leadership effectiveness, team dynamics, and overall organizational culture?

_____

_____

_____

TIP 76:
DEVELOP EFFECTIVE CRISIS COMMUNICATION SKILLS

Develop effective crisis communication skills to convey information, address concerns, and maintain trust during crises or challenging situations. Be transparent, timely, and compassionate in your communications. Listen actively, provide accurate information, and demonstrate empathy. Developing these crisis communication skills will enable you to manage reputational risks and preserve stakeholder trust.

How can developing effective crisis communication skills help you to navigate crises, maintain stakeholder trust, and protect your organization's reputation?

_____

_____

_____

TIP 77:
CULTIVATE SYSTEMS THINKING

Cultivate systems thinking by understanding the interconnectedness of various components within a complex system. Consider the ripple effects of actions and decisions, identify feedback loops, and analyze the broader context. Cultivating systems thinking enhances your ability to solve complex problems, make informed decisions, and drive systemic change.

How can cultivating systems thinking enhance your problem-solving abilities, promote innovation, and drive positive change within your organization?

_____

_____

_____

TIP 78:

FOSTER KNOWLEDGE SHARING
AND COLLABORATION

Foster knowledge sharing and collaboration by creating platforms and processes that facilitate the exchange of ideas, insights, and expertise. Encourage employees to share knowledge. Recognize and reward collaboration, and create a culture that values collective intelligence. Fostering knowledge sharing and collaboration enhances organizational learning, innovation, and overall performance.

How can you foster knowledge sharing and collaboration to promote learning, improve problem-solving, and drive organizational success?

_____

_____

_____

TIP 79:
DEVELOP EFFECTIVE VIRTUAL COLLABORATION SKILLS

Develop effective virtual collaboration skills to work efficiently with others in a remote or virtual setting. Use collaboration tools, establish clear communication channels, and foster a sense of connection and engagement. Adapt your collaboration techniques to the virtual environment, and cultivate trust and effective teamwork. Developing virtual collaboration skills enhances productivity, strengthens relationships, and drives successful outcomes in remote work scenarios.

How can you develop effective virtual collaboration skills to promote teamwork, maintain engagement, and achieve shared goals in a remote work environment?

_____

_____

TIP 80:

FOSTER PSYCHOLOGICAL SAFETY

Foster psychological safety by creating an environment where individuals feel safe to speak up, share ideas, and take risks without fear of judgment or retribution. Encourage open communication, listen actively, and respond constructively to feedback. Fostering psychological safety nurtures innovation, enhances collaboration, and supports individual and team growth.

How can you foster psychological safety within your team or organization to create a culture that encourages open communication, learning, and innovation?

_____

_____

_____

TIP 81:
LEAD WITH CULTURAL SENSITIVITY

Lead with cultural sensitivity by understanding and respecting cultural norms, values, and practices. Adapt your leadership approach to accommodate diverse cultural backgrounds and perspectives. Embrace diversity, promote inclusion, and foster cultural awareness among your team or organization. Leading with cultural sensitivity builds trust, fosters inclusion, and drives high-performing teams.

How can you lead with cultural sensitivity to bridge cultural gaps, create an inclusive environment, and promote collaboration across diverse teams?

_____

_____

_____

TIP 82:

DEVELOP RESILIENT CHANGE LEADERSHIP SKILLS

Develop resilient change leadership skills to effectively lead and manage change within your team or organization. Anticipate and address resistance, communicate the need for change, and provide support throughout the change process. Foster resilience among team members and promote a growth mindset. Developing resilient change leadership skills enables you to navigate uncertainty, inspire others, and drive successful change initiatives.

How can developing resilient change leadership skills help you to lead and manage change effectively, inspire your team, and achieve successful outcomes?

_____

_____

TIP 83:
FOSTER EMPOWERMENT AND ACCOUNTABILITY

Foster empowerment and accountability by delegating authority, providing autonomy, and encouraging individuals to take ownership of their work. Set clear expectations, provide support, and hold individuals accountable for their actions and outcomes. Fostering empowerment and accountability cultivates a sense of ownership, enhances motivation, and drives individual and team performance.

How can you foster empowerment and accountability within your team or organization to drive performance, promote growth, and achieve desired outcomes?

_____

_____

_____

TIP 84:
DEVELOP EFFECTIVE CONFLICT
RESOLUTION SKILLS

Develop effective conflict resolution skills to address conflicts in a constructive and timely manner. Actively listen to all perspectives, seek win-win solutions, and use mediation techniques. Manage emotions and encourage open dialogue. Developing these skills will help you to create a positive and harmonious work environment.

How can developing effective conflict resolution skills help you to navigate conflicts, promote understanding, and foster positive relationships within your team or organization?

_____

_____

_____

TIP 85:
CULTIVATE SELF-ADVOCACY AND EMOTIONAL WELL-BEING

Cultivate the practice of self-advocacy and prioritize your emotional well-being when faced with negative treatment from others. Recognize the importance of stating how you feel, setting boundaries, and standing up for yourself in a respectful and assertive manner. Valuing your feelings and advocating for yourself fosters healthy relationships and creates a positive environment around you.

How can you cultivate the practice of self-advocacy and prioritize your emotional well-being when dealing with people who treat you in a negative manner?

_____

_____

_____

TIP 86:

FOSTER RESILIENCE IN TIMES OF CHANGE

Foster resilience in times of change by helping individuals adapt, cope, and thrive in the face of challenges and uncertainty. Provide support, communicate openly, and help individuals develop resilience strategies. Foster a positive and supportive environment that encourages growth and learning. Fostering resilience in times of change enables individuals to bounce back, embrace opportunities, and achieve personal and professional growth.

How can you foster resilience in individuals during times of change to help them navigate challenges, embrace growth opportunities, and maintain their well-being?

_____

_____

_____

TIP 87:
LEAD WITH SOCIAL RESPONSIBILITY

Lead with social responsibility by considering the impact of your decisions and actions on society, the environment, and future generations. Embrace sustainability, corporate social responsibility, and ethical practices. Promote initiatives that contribute to the well-being of communities and the planet. Leading with social responsibility creates a positive impact, enhances your reputation, and drives long-term sustainable success.

How can you lead with social responsibility to create a positive impact, drive sustainability, and contribute to the betterment of society?

_____

_____

_____

TIP 88:

EMBRACE QUALITY FAMILY TIME AND PRIORITIZE MEANINGFUL CONNECTIONS

Embrace the importance of quality family time and make it a priority to foster meaningful connections with your loved ones. Recognize that spending time with family is a source of joy, love, and support in your life. Evaluate your commitments and ensure that you allocate dedicated time for family activities, conversations, and shared experiences. Embracing quality family time strengthens relationships, creates lasting memories, and enriches your overall well-being.

How can you proactively embrace quality family time and prioritize meaningful connections with your loved ones, ensuring that you create cherished memories and nurture your family relationships?

TIP 89:

PROMOTE WORKFORCE DIVERSITY

Promote workforce diversity by actively seeking diverse talents, promoting equal opportunities, and creating an inclusive environment. Embrace diversity of gender, race, ethnicity, age, background, and perspectives. Foster a culture that values and celebrates diversity. Promoting workforce diversity enhances creativity, innovation, and organizational performance.

How can you promote workforce diversity to create an inclusive and equitable workplace that values diverse perspectives and fosters innovation?

_____

_____

_____

TIP 90:

CULTIVATE INTERPERSONAL EFFECTIVENESS

Cultivate interpersonal effectiveness by developing strong communication, empathy, and relationship-building skills. Practice active listening, adapt your communication style, and build rapport with others. Develop emotional intelligence and interpersonal sensitivity. Cultivating interpersonal effectiveness enhances your ability to connect with others, resolve conflicts, and build positive relationships.

How can cultivating interpersonal effectiveness positively impact your communication, relationships, and efficiency in personal and professional settings?

_____

_____

_____

TIP 91:
DEVELOP AGILITY AND ADAPTABILITY

Develop agility and adaptability to thrive in fast-paced and ever-changing environments. Embrace change, seek opportunities for growth, and remain flexible in your thinking and approach. Develop the ability to quickly adapt to new circumstances and learn from experiences. Agility and adaptability will allow you to navigate uncertainty, seize opportunities, and drive personal and organizational success.

How can you develop agility and adaptability to effectively respond to change, seize opportunities, and achieve personal and professional growth?

_____

_____

_____

TIP 92:

SHARE YOUR STORY: YOUR VOICE MATTERS

Recognize the power of your unique story and the impact it can have on others. Share your experiences, perspectives, and insights with authenticity and courage. Your voice matters, and by sharing your story, you can inspire, educate, and connect with others on a deeper level. Embrace the opportunity to make a difference through your personal narrative.

How can you embrace the power of your own story and find opportunities to share it with others to make a positive impact?

_____

_____

_____

TIP 93:
FOSTER INNOVATION AND
CREATIVITY IN TEAMS

Foster innovation and creativity in teams by creating a culture that encourages new ideas and risk-taking. Provide resources, time, and support for innovative projects. Embrace diverse perspectives, celebrate failures as learning opportunities, and reward creativity. Fostering innovation and creativity drives continuous improvement, sparks innovation, and promotes a culture of ingenuity.

How can you foster innovation and creativity in teams to drive breakthrough solutions, foster a culture of continuous improvement, and achieve exceptional results?

_____

_____

_____

TIP 94:
DEVELOP CULTURAL AGILITY

Develop cultural agility by developing the knowledge, skills, and attitudes needed to effectively interact and work with individuals from different cultural backgrounds. Seek to understand diverse cultural norms, values, and communication styles. Embrace cultural differences, adapt your behavior, and demonstrate respect and openness. Developing cultural agility enhances your ability to collaborate globally, build inclusive teams, and drive international success.

How can you develop cultural agility to effectively work with individuals from diverse cultural backgrounds and promote global collaboration and understanding?

_____

_____

_____

TIP 95:
PROMOTE WORK-LIFE INTEGRATION

Promote work-life integration by fostering a supportive work environment that encourages balance, flexibility, and well-being. Provide opportunities for work-life integration, promote self-care, and encourage healthy boundaries. Support employees in achieving a harmonious blend of work and personal life. Promoting work-life integration enhances employee satisfaction, well-being, and overall work performance.

How can you promote work-life integration within your team or organization to support employee well-being, satisfaction, and productivity?

_____

_____

_____

Part VI:

SELF- REFLECTION AND PERSONAL GROWTH

TIP 96:

CULTIVATE A GROWTH MINDSET CULTURE

Cultivate a growth mindset culture by encouraging continuous learning, embracing challenges, and celebrating effort and growth. Foster a belief that abilities can be developed through dedication and hard work. Provide feedback that promotes growth, encourage risk-taking, and create a safe environment for making mistakes and learning from them. By cultivating a growth mindset culture, you can promote resilience, innovation, and personal and organizational development.

How can you cultivate a growth mindset culture within your team or organization to foster resilience, learning, and continuous improvement?

_____

_____

_____

TIP 97:

LEAD WITH AUTHENTICITY AND INCLUSION

Lead with authenticity and inclusion by creating an environment where individuals feel valued, respected, and included. Be genuine, promote diversity, and ensure equal opportunities for all. Embrace individual differences, foster a sense of belonging, and challenge biases. Leading with authenticity and inclusion creates a culture of trust, respect, and empowerment.

How can you lead with authenticity and inclusion to create an inclusive work environment that values diversity, fosters belonging, and promotes collaboration?

_____

_____

_____

TIP 98:
DARE TO BE DIFFERENT

Have the courage to dare to be different and create what does not exist. Break free from the conventional norms and explore innovative ideas. Embrace your uniqueness and let your creativity soar. By daring to be different, you have the power to shape new possibilities and leave a lasting impact.

How can you cultivate the courage to step outside the boundaries of conformity and create something truly unique and groundbreaking?

_____

_____

_____

Tip 99:
Cultivate Effective Change Management Skills

Cultivate effective change management skills to navigate and lead change successfully within your team or organization. Understand the change process, communicate effectively, and address resistance and challenges. Provide support and resources, and create a culture that embraces change and fosters resilience. Cultivating these change management skills will enable you to lead change initiatives, engage stakeholders, and drive successful organizational transformation.

How can you cultivate effective change management skills to lead and manage change effectively, engage your team, and achieve successful outcomes?

_____

_____

TIP 100:
DEVELOP EFFECTIVE
PROBLEM-SOLVING SKILLS

Develop effective problem-solving skills to identify, analyze, and resolve complex challenges.
Embrace a systematic approach, gather relevant
information, consider multiple perspectives, and
generate innovative solutions. Developing effective problem-solving skills, such as critical thinking and decision-making abilities, enhances your
ability to overcome obstacles, make sound decisions, and achieve desired outcomes.

How can you develop effective problem-solving
skills to enhance your ability to tackle complex
challenges and make informed decisions for successful outcomes?

TIP 101:
EMBRACE YOUR UNIQUE VOICE

Embrace your unique voice and perspective. Dare to be different, share your authentic ideas, and express yourself authentically. Your unique voice brings new perspectives and creativity to the world. Celebrate your individuality and have the courage to stand out and make a difference.

How can you embrace your unique voice and express yourself authentically to make a positive impact in the world?

_____

_____

_____

TIP 102:
EMBRACE COURAGEOUS LEADERSHIP THROUGH ACTIVE LISTENING

Embracing courageous leadership entails practicing and promoting active listening within your teams and organizations. By genuinely hearing and understanding the perspectives of others, leaders can build trust, encourage open dialogue, and gain valuable insights. Active listening demonstrates respect, creates a supportive environment, and enhances problem-solving and decision-making.

How can you, as a leader, embrace courageous leadership by fostering increased active listening and creating a culture of collaboration, empathy, and effective problem-solving within your teams and organization? What actions can you take to demonstrate your commitment to active listening and encourage others to do the same?

Tip 103:
Be an Upstander, Not a Bystander

Observing people being treated poorly or unfairly and remaining silent makes you complicit in the problem. Instead, choose to be an upstander and take a stand against injustice or mistreatment. Speak up for what is right, advocate for those who are marginalized or mistreated, and foster a culture of respect and inclusion. Refrain from participating in gossip or spreading rumors, as this perpetuates negativity and undermines trust. By being an upstander, you contribute to a positive and supportive environment.

How can you actively practice being an upstander and create a culture where mistreatment is not tolerated? What steps can you take to encourage others to join you in standing up against injustice and fostering a culture of respect and support?

SELF-DIRECTED REFLECTION
AND PERSONAL GROWTH

Enhancing communication is the most powerful tool for shared understanding to enhance the world. Congratulations on acquiring 103 tips to enhance your personal and professional development! With this comprehensive collection of insights, you now have a toolkit that can be utilized in various ways. Whether you're looking to break the ice, spark engaging table topics, facilitate group discussions, or initiate a journey of self-reflection and journaling, these tips provide a foundation to explore and implement effective techniques.

One powerful method to leverage the wisdom contained within these tips is through round-table discussions. By gathering a group of individuals who are eager to learn and grow, you can foster insightful conversations that encourage collaboration, shared experiences, and collective wisdom. The following questions can serve as excellent conversation starters, igniting meaningful discussions and promoting personal and professional growth.

Additionally, these prompts can be used for individual reflection. Taking the time to contemplate these questions in solitude will allow for deeper introspection and self-discovery. Use them as a guide to explore your own thoughts, values, and aspirations, and uncover new insights about yourself and your leadership journey.

Remember, the power of these prompts lies in your willingness to engage with them authentically. Embrace the opportunity for self-directed reflection and personal growth, and let these questions guide you toward new perspectives, ideas, and self-discovery.

Now, without further ado, let's look into a list of thought-provoking prompts and questions. May they inspire meaningful conversations, ignite personal insights, and guide you on a transformative journey of self-improvement and leadership development.

1. Reflect on an unspoken truth in your leadership journey that has shaped your decisions.
2. What unspoken truth about power dynamics do you believe every leader should acknowledge?
3. How can acknowledging your personal weaknesses as a leader impact your leadership style?
4. Discuss the role of transparency in addressing unspoken truths in leadership.
5. Write about an unspoken truth in leadership that you learned the hard way.
6. How can embracing unspoken truths foster innovation in leadership?
7. What is an unspoken truth about employee motivation that leaders often overlook?
8. Analyze the role of emotional intelligence in uncovering unspoken truths among team members.
9. Take time to reflect on a time when acknowledging an unspoken truth improved team morale.

10. How can recognizing the unspoken truths of the market impact business strategies?

11. What unspoken truths in organizational culture do leaders need to address for long-term success?

12. Discuss the importance of confronting personal biases as a leader.

13. How can acknowledging unspoken truths improve your ability to make decisions under pressure?

14. Write about an unspoken truth regarding work-life balance in leadership positions.

15. Discuss how acknowledging unspoken truths can make a leader more approachable.

16. How can embracing the unspoken truth of constant change make you a more adaptive leader?

17. Explore the role of humility in addressing unspoken truths as a leader.

18. What is an unspoken truth about networking that you believe is crucial for leaders?

19. Discuss the impact of unspoken truths on a

leader's ability to manage conflicts.

20. How can a leader's willingness to address unspoken truths affect their legacy?

21. Reflect on how unspoken truths in global politics can influence international business leadership.

22. How can acknowledging unspoken truths enhance a leader's ability to mentor others?

23. Describe how listening skills can help a leader uncover unspoken truths.

24. How do unspoken truths about failure shape a leader's resilience?

25. Discuss the role of intuition in recognizing unspoken truths in decision-making.

26. How can acknowledging unspoken truths improve delegation skills?

27. What is an unspoken truth about diversity and inclusion that leaders should embrace?

28. Explore the relationship between ethics and unspoken truths in leadership.

29. Reflect on how understanding unspoken truths in negotiation can make you a better

leader.

30. Discuss the unspoken truth of the impact of mental health on leadership effectiveness.

31. How can acknowledging the unspoken truths of others' perspectives improve collaboration?

32. Write about the importance of addressing unspoken truths in times of organizational crisis.

33. How do unspoken truths in your industry shape leadership challenges and opportunities?

34. What unspoken truth about personal development is essential for leadership growth?

35. Describe how embracing unspoken truths can aid in succession planning and leadership transitions.

36. Explore how self-awareness can help leaders recognize unspoken truths within themselves.

37. How can acknowledging unspoken truths about resource limitations improve strategic planning?

38. Discuss the unspoken truths regarding the expectations and realities of leadership roles.

39. Analyze how leadership styles can either reveal or conceal unspoken truths.

40. Reflect on how unspoken truths can affect trust within an organization.

41. How can understanding unspoken truths of customer behavior shape leadership in marketing?

42. Discuss how embracing unspoken truths can contribute to corporate social responsibility.

43. How can leaders address unspoken truths without causing unnecessary tension?

44. What is the role of vulnerability in acknowledging unspoken truths as a leader?

45. Discuss how understanding the unspoken truths of competitors can be beneficial.

46. How can acknowledging unspoken truths enhance your ability to handle feedback and criticism?

47. Explore the relationship between organizational core values and unspoken truths.

48. How do unspoken truths about different leadership styles affect team dynamics?

49. Analyze the role of unspoken truths in change management and organizational transformation.

50. Reflect on how recognizing unspoken truths can help in talent acquisition and retention.

51. How can a leader address the unspoken truth that not all decisions will please everyone?

52. Discuss the importance of acknowledging the unspoken truth of burnout in leadership.

53. Explore how understanding unspoken truths can enhance customer relations and services.

54. Reflect on the role of unspoken truths in strategic partnerships and alliances.

55. How can embracing unspoken truths about oneself bolster one's personal leadership brand?

56. Discuss how leaders can encourage a culture where unspoken truths are shared openly.

57. Explore the role of cultural sensitivity in understanding unspoken truths in international

leadership.

58. Reflect on the unspoken truth that some relationships within the team may require more effort.

59. Discuss the balance between being authoritative and embracing unspoken truths as a leader.

60. How can understanding the unspoken truths of generational differences impact leadership?

61. Explore the role of passion and motivation in addressing unspoken truths as a leader.

62. Discuss how technology can reveal unspoken truths that impact leadership decisions.

63. Write about how leaders can ensure that addressing unspoken truths does not lead to negativity.

64. Analyze how unspoken truths can shape a leader's crisis communication strategy.

65. How can acknowledging unspoken truths help in setting more realistic goals?

66. Discuss the importance of leaders being able

to recognize when unspoken truths signal a need for change.

67. How can understanding the unspoken truths of employee aspirations impact talent development?

68. Explore the role of authenticity in addressing unspoken truths as a leader.

69. Reflect on how leaders can avoid letting unspoken truths create blind spots.

70. How can leaders ensure that they address unspoken truths ethically?

71. Discuss how leaders can foster an environment where unspoken truths are not stigmatized.

72. How can leaders balance intuition and data in understanding unspoken truths?

73. Reflect on the role of unspoken truths in creating and maintaining a leadership vision.

74. Explore how leaders can use unspoken truths to strengthen organizational culture.

75. Discuss the unspoken truths of fostering innovation and creativity within a team.

76. How can acknowledging unspoken truths about market trends benefit business leaders?

77. Reflect on the unspoken truths that leaders must embrace in the face of adversity.

78. How can leaders address unspoken truths to foster a more inclusive work environment?

79. Explore the impact of unspoken truths on a leader's personal and professional relationships.

80. Discuss how leaders can maintain morale while addressing uncomfortable unspoken truths.

81. How can leaders address the unspoken truth that sometimes hard decisions have to be made for the greater good?

82. Discuss how leaders can constructively address unspoken truths that arise from rumors and misinformation.

83. Reflect on the unspoken truths that leaders must navigate when considering mergers or acquisitions.

84. Explore how leaders can manage the unspo-

ken expectations of shareholders or stakeholders.

85. Discuss how leaders can address the unspoken truths of evolving customer needs.

86. Reflect on how unspoken truths can shape a
leader's personal and professional legacy.

87. How can leaders ensure that the process of
addressing unspoken truths is continuous and
not just a one-time action?

88. Discuss how leaders can prepare themselves
mentally to address unspoken truths.

89. Explore how leaders can utilize mentors or
coaches to understand and address unspoken
truths.

90. Reflect on how embracing unspoken truths
can contribute to a leader's ability to inspire
others.

91. How can understanding unspoken truths contribute to a leader's conflict resolution skills?

92. Discuss how leaders can address the unspoken truths of remote or hybrid working environments.

93. Reflect on how embracing unspoken truths can impact a leader's negotiation skills.

94. Discuss how leaders can use unspoken truths to build bridges between departments or teams.

95. How can leaders address the unspoken truths surrounding mental health in the workplace?

96. Explore the role of unspoken truths in building and maintaining a leader's credibility.

97. Reflect on how leaders can use unspoken truths to manage and overcome bias in decision-making.

98. Discuss how leaders can cultivate a culture of accountability by addressing unspoken truths.

99. Reflect on how acknowledging unspoken truths can affect a leader's personal well-being and self-care.

100. How can leaders develop a systematic approach to uncovering, understanding, and addressing unspoken truths in their organizations?

101. How can leaders continue to apply the

knowledge gained from exploring unspoken truths in their leadership journey?

A Personal Note from Katherine

One of the most powerful truths we can embrace is the importance of being honest with ourselves. We all have moments when we try to convince ourselves that everything is fine, even when deep down we know it's not. But this self-deception only holds us back from reaching our full potential.

It takes courage to acknowledge when something is wrong and to face the truth head-on. By being true to ourselves, we open the door to growth, personal transformation, and living a more authentic life.

Remember, it's okay to admit our flaws, acknowledge our mistakes, and confront the challenges we face. Embracing our truth allows us to break free and step into a future where we can fully become who we are meant to be. Never stop trying or evolving. Learning occurs each day.

So, let us commit to being true to ourselves,

embracing the unspoken truth that resides within us, and forging a path toward personal fulfillment and authenticity. Be your true authentic self. Together, we can create a life that aligns with our deepest values and aspirations.

With love and encouragement.
— *Dr. Katherine Y. Brown*

Connect on Social Media:

Facebook.com/DrKatherineBrown
Twitter.com/KatherineyBrown
LinkedIn.com/in/katherineybrown
Instagram.com/drkatherineybrown

JOURNAL